The Strong Staff broken, and the Beautiful Rod:

A

DISCOURSE

DELIVERED BEFORE THE

MEMBERS OF THE SECOND PARISH IN WORCESTER,

ON THE OCCASION OF THE DEATH OF THE

HON. JOHN WALDO LINCOLN,

WHO DIED OCT. 2, 1852.

BY ALONZO HILL,

PASTOR OF THE SECOND CHURCH.

BOSTON:
PRINTED BY JOHN WILSON & SON,
22, SCHOOL STREET.
1852.

Worcester, Oct. 14, 1852.

Rev. Dr. Hill.

Dear Sir, — I have been accidentally prevented making this communication, which I had intended several days since. I beg now to express to you my most cordial, heartfelt acknowledgments for your impressive, interesting, and eloquent tribute to the character and memory of my late beloved Brother, in your Sermon of the last Sabbath; and earnestly and respectfully to request, that you would permit me to cause it to be printed under your own supervision. There are many who will be gratified by its perusal, besides those who had the satisfaction to hear it. It was most truthful and just in its biographical notice, and would be grateful to his friends as a fitting record of the virtues it commemorates. I pray you to believe me deeply sensible to the obligation I am under for your unfailing sympathy and kindness.

With the most faithful esteem and respect,

I am, dear Sir,

Your Friend, Parishioner, and obedient Servant,

LEVI LINCOLN.

DISCOURSE.

Jeremiah xlviii. 17. — ALL YE THAT ARE ABOUT HIM, BEMOAN HIM; AND ALL YE THAT KNOW HIS NAME, SAY, HOW IS THE STRONG STAFF BROKEN, AND THE BEAUTIFUL ROD!

As I read these words, I feel sure that you at once comprehend their meaning, and readily apply them. They suggest the union of strength and beauty of character; and his image is in all our hearts to-day, to honor whose remains a great company came here the last week, whose look of sorrow still fastens on our memories, and whose parting footsteps still linger on our ears. They who were about him, and they who knew his name, say with ourselves, — How is the strong staff broken, and the beautiful rod!

In olden days, in the East, the staff was the emblem of royal power, and the rod of royal clemency; and, when these two were bound together, and, like the Roman fasces, borne before the magistracy, they indicated a combination of strength and tenderness, — the leading attributes of all genuine royalty. Without resorting to the language of poetry, they still indicate the two elements which enter into the composition of all who are born to control other men, and leave a permanent mark upon their times. With either alone, the character is essentially defective. With strength only, a man may make himself felt; but that which he accomplishes is by force, compelling a reluctant submission and an unwilling obedience. He controls through the pains which he inflicts, or the fears which he awakens; and rears monuments in the pathway oftener than grateful memories in the hearts of men. It is the power by which despots reign; and, whether residing in castle-walls, in armed battalia, or in an invincible will, it is solitary in its nature; it gathers no sympathies around it; it cuts off its possessor from his kind, and depresses and crushes while it rules.

So also, on the other hand, gentleness and clemency alone will not form an exalted character. A man may do all things with charity, with the best feeling and purpose, but do them very feebly. How often do we hear it said of another, "He is a very good man; he is very kind and tender-hearted," when it is meant all the while that he is a very weak man. His heart may beat with sympathy, his bosom may overflow with affection, and his hands may be opened for every good work; but, lacking inward power, strength of will, purpose and principle, he accomplishes little or no good. He belongs to that harmless but inefficient class, of whom it may be said, if they have not guided the world's destinies, they have not added to the world's woes; by their cheerfulness and good nature, they may have added to its satisfactions.

But alone, neither of these qualities will suffice. There must be a union of energy and tenderness, — the staff of strength and the rod of beauty, if we would accomplish any thing really permanent and good. They may be variously, and in different proportions, combined: the one or the other may predominate; but they must both enter into the composition of him who acts a part any way distinguished on the theatre of life. The clear mind and the strong will, the warm heart and the tender conscience, — these are the elements that go to make the genuine man, whom we love and trust while he lives, and for whom we mourn when he is dead.

No one will doubt that these qualities of which we have been speaking were the leading attributes of his character, who, for more than forty years, has been so intimately associated with the welfare of our city and county; whose influence we have felt in so many relations, and whose perishing body paused here the other day, as it was on its way to his own sepulchre in our beautiful cemetery to enjoy that repose which he so well earned, and which shall never be disturbed by the hand of man. In him were prostrated the strong staff and the beautiful rod, — the energy and affectionateness which go to make the man of mark. That they were his leading characteristics, we can see and comprehend; but in what proportions they were combined, what manner of man he was, what good traits distinguished him, what lasting services he rendered, what there was in him worthy of remembrance and imitation, — many of us, who did not know him intimately, may wish to learn. There is an infinite diversity in the character of good men; and human excellence ever comes to us in new combinations, in novel and ever-varied forms. No one is perfect, — no one embraces in himself all that is highest and best; but no man can, for so many years, have been so trusted and honored, and, now he is dead, have been so mourned, without possessing traits of excellence, noble and beautiful features of character, which, for the sake of justice to our own minds and hearts, for the sake of the incitement and moral quickening which they afford, and for the sake of the example which they present, we ought to gather up, and hold up to our view. It is the mark of little minds to dwell on human frailty; it is Christian to contemplate with a frank and generous appreciation whatever is true and honest, and worthy of good report. In order, then, that you may perceive in what proportions the noble and beautiful traits of his character were combined, what circumstances contributed to make him the man he was, and what services he has rendered in his day, — let us contemplate some of the leading events of his outward life. We shall learn why he held such a conspicuous place in public estimation, and we obtain a more just appreciation of the strength and tenderness that were in him. I believe him to be worthy of a public notice from this place. I believe him to have been a trustworthy and thoroughly good man. If I did not, no eminence of station, no length or amount of public service, could induce me to speak of him at this season of our solemnities, when man and his deeds should be forgotten in the grander contemplation of God and Christ and eternity.

John Waldo Lincoln, third son of the late Hon. Levi Lincoln, and brother of the Hon. Levi Lincoln, late Governor of Massachusetts, and of the late Hon. Enoch Lincoln, Governor of Maine, was born in this town, June 21, 1787; and was baptized by my venerable predecessor, 8th of July following. He received no other education than that which he obtained under the parental roof, and at the public schools in this place. In consequence of an early and marked impediment in his speech, which was deemed a bar to his success in either of the professions, he was compelled to forego the advantages of a collegiate course, to renounce the idea of that professional life to which his family seemed born and were destined, and devote himself to business. And here in the very beginning, in connection with his infirmity, we find an illustration of those qualities which were his most striking characteristics. He submitted to the necessity without a murmur, with the loss of none of the sweetness and affectionateness of his nature. Not only so, but, through energy and perseverance, he so entirely overcame the defect, so obtained the mastery of his organs, in private and in public, that no one would have suspected his early infirmity, if tradition had not preserved the memory of it.

At the age of fourteen, he became an apprentice in the store of his relative, the late Hon. Daniel Waldo, whose strict habits of business, whose unwavering integrity and hearty personal interest in the inmates of his shop, had a marked influence upon their character. This worthy man, unable to escape the feelings of personal responsibleness for those entrusted to his guardianship, could not satisfy his high notions of duty merely by the fulfilment of the required service during the hours of business, but, according to the good customs of those days, made them the inmates of his own family, and the sharers of his domestic pleasures; and, as there are living witnesses to testify, followed them in their inexperience and early conflicts, with an interest that never abated, and a prompt kindness that was never exhausted. In such a school Mr. Lincoln was faithfully taught. He incurred obligations of respect and affection, which subsequent years were too short to repay. He acquired habits of order which never forsook him, and a readiness in and devotion to business which followed him to the day of his death.

After terminating his apprenticeship, he opened a store on his own account in this place. But at that period there were public interests which engrossed the public mind, and absorbed all private concerns. We were in the midst of the war of 1812; and in all our homes were anxiety and distress, of which the present generation cannot adequately conceive; for war waged on our borders with the most powerful nation on the globe is a very different thing from war carried on with a feeble people, on their own soil, at the distance of half the continent. The channels of intercourse were interrupted, the avenues of industry were stopped, ships were rotting in our harbors, and hundreds of families were cut off from the usual means of subsistence. Ruin stared our people in the face, and gloom and despondency hung over their minds. English ships of war hovered around our coasts, were seen from our headlands, and threatened to bombard our cities. An actual invasion of Boston was seriously apprehended, and a requisition was made on the military companies of the interior to hasten to its defence. Col. Lincoln was at that time the Commander of the Light Infantry of this town. With energy and almost unequalled despatch, he, with his command, was already on his march; but not, as they believed, to any holiday review. It was a mustering for a more serious work. And, that we may learn how seriously it was regarded, we need only be told that it was a sabbath morning, and solemn divine service was held in presence of the company on the day of their departure; and again, on their return six weeks after, in the same public manner, there was an offering of public thanks, as if they had escaped some dread and imminent peril. On this occasion, our fellow-townsman particularly distinguished himself for his zeal, activity, and devotion, and won for himself the confidence and personal regards of the Executive of the Commonwealth.

In 1824, Col. Lincoln was chosen Representative to the General Court, and, in 1825, one of the Selectmen of the town; and, from that time to the day of his death, almost without interruption, he was engaged in the service of the town, county, or commonwealth, or all. Representative for four years, he became a Senator, and served as many more. In both branches of the Legislature, we are told that "he was ever regarded as one of the best of all the members, for practical ability, sound judgment, and unfaltering fidelity to the public interests." In the county, he was for many years the Chairman of the Board of Commissioners; and we are indebted to no one more than to him for the spacious and well-adapted highways that diverge from our city, and afford facilities of intercourse between village and village. He was the projector of the canal which connected our city with the ocean; and which, though now yielding to better means of communication, contributed essentially to our early prosperity. He was for seven years the High Sheriff of the county; and, during all this period, there was a confidence, a sense of protection in his well-known promptness and energy, that was never for a moment shaken. Whatever might threaten from the boldness of evil-doers and the turbulence of human passion, all looked to his well-tried courage, and felt assured that his presence, and a word from his lips, would quell the tumult of excitement, and restore peace. The reckless offender quailed before his calm eye; and, though he had hitherto defied the law, he retired from its minister now, alarmed and rebuked. As the President of an Insurance Company, as the Director of a Bank and Railroad Company, and as a Municipal Officer, he was trusted, because he was ever found competent and faithful. It was not safe to call in question the wisdom of his measures, for it was not easy to propose better; and it would have been base to charge him with sacrificing the least public interest to a private end, or with turning a hair's-breadth from the line of duty for a party purpose; for I am confident, that, in all his public relations, he was above suspicion, as he was above reproach; and that, by common acknowledgment, a more able, faithful, and devoted public servant has not been among us.

But I pass over these, though men of affairs find in his habits of business much to commend, and speak of the amount of his public services with fond affection. I dwell upon two or three examples of his wise forecast and disinterested devotion to the public welfare, the results, if not the labors, of which you can appreciate.

Col. Lincoln was, at the time of his death, the President of the Agricultural Society of this county. This fact will indicate the direction of his tastes, and the appreciation in which he was held. From early manhood, he took pleasure in the labors of husbandry, and loved to steal away from the confinement of the office, the counting-house, and the court-room, to commune with nature in her milder aspects, and find relief and gratification in watching the varied productions of field and orchard, from early springtime to latest harvest. He loved to look on the meadows which had been reclaimed, and the hill-sides which waved with the standing grain. He loved to be the owner of fine cattle, both great and small, and to contemplate improved breeds, of large and fairest proportions. Nor was he a mere observer only: he was an experimenter also. He sought to make his farm a model farm. He furnished himself with a choice collection of agricultural books; he craved knowledge near and from afar; he introduced the improvements of others; he made improvements of his own; and there was no one who hailed with more satisfaction, or contributed more substantial aid to, the progress of all that relates to good husbandry. In the promotion of its interests, he spared no labor, and grudged no expense; and so competent was he deemed, that one of the last services to which he was appointed was that of Commissioner on the Board of Agriculture recently established in this Commonwealth. And so it was that the Agricultural Society, over which he was called to preside, was an object of his pride and affection. He dwelt with fond satisfaction on the good which it had accomplished, on the encouragement which it had afforded the husbandman in his labors, and the more abundant harvests with which it had rewarded them. And he looked forward with sanguine expectation to the still more extended usefulness of the Association. Its interests were very dear to him; and, amid the pains of a wasting sickness, his ever-active brain was teeming with plans for the advancement of its prosperity. A little incident will illustrate the habits of his mind, as well as his devotion to this object. A short time before his death, a parcel of land had been purchased for the use of the Society. It was a consummation which he had devoutly desired, and which afforded him very sincere gratification. But scarcely had the grateful news reached his ears, when at once, without a moment's delay, without leaving the desk at which he sat, he drew a plan of the building which he conceived should be erected on it, and was impatient to see the work already begun. In this cause, as in every other, he possessed not a little of that prompt energy so admired in the African traveller, who, when asked at what early day he would commence his voyage of discovery, replied, "To-morrow." Col. Lincoln loved the profession whose interests he had espoused: it fell in with his settled tastes. He saw a good to be accomplished, and he could not brook delay. And was he not right? Is not improvement in our fields and flocks a positive good and a positive gain on the score of human happiness? It may seem a small thing, scarcely worth the pains, to make one spire of grass grow where none grew before, or to make the acre yield two where it only yielded one measure before; but times and changing seasons justify the expenditure, and proclaim the greatness of the benefaction. She who first carried a handful of wheat into Europe may have seemed to do no great thing in her day; but she is now acknowledged as the benefactress to her race by the wavings of a thousand wheat-fields, and by the echoes of a thousand harvest homes. Mary Stuart was not noticed when she bore a willow wand from her beloved France to Scotland; but that one act is now commemorated in a hundred quiet nooks, and finds fitting memorial in the grateful shade which falls upon Scotland's dead in a hundred village grave-yards. And is not he worthy of being remembered, who, not only in one but in multiplied ways, for half a century, has endeavored to lighten the labors of the husbandman, — has sought out and brought for his use the fairest of the field and flock, compelled our sterile soil to be fruitful, and scattered abundance and grace and beauty all around? Col. Lincoln has done something for a cause that was dear to him. Let me add, he meditated much more. Had he been spared in health and vigor, I have reason to know that he would have been foremost in securing schools of agriculture, which, if they ever be established, will elevate the mechanical occupation of the farmer into a science, and give it a first place among the liberal sciences.

Another object that deeply interested the mind and heart of Col. Lincoln was the moral condition of the inmates of our prisons. The philanthropy of our times had not utterly neglected and forsaken this portion of our race. The prisons of New England had ceased, to a large extent, to be schools of depravity, — the dark, damp, dreary places, where hope never came that comes to all. Benevolent individuals had, from time to time, found their way into them; means of moral and religious culture had been occasionally afforded the inmates; but to him are we pre-eminently indebted for the first instance of a county prison in which the chaplain was one of the constituted officers, and in which moral and religious instruction was statedly given at the public expense. Such an office had existed, and such instruction had been given, in the State Penitentiary, where convicts, perhaps hardened in crime, are confined for a long period of years. Col. Lincoln was the first to see what a chaplaincy might accomplish under other and more favorable circumstances. He was the first to perceive that the young offender, whose cheek yet mantled with shame at the thought of a first offence, who yet remembered his early home and the lessons of his childhood, and in whom the desire of being good had not all died out, — he was the first to perceive, that such a one, kindly visited in the solitude of his cell, and tenderly entreated in the sabbath lesson, might be greatly benefited, perhaps reclaimed, by the labors of a permanent ministry in the place. Wisely and well he judged; for, under the wholesome influences now brought within its walls, our prison has become, what Latimer once said of the English prisons, when they were crowded with English confessors and martyrs, "a right good school of Christian piety." It has become, I am sure, a school of reform. I know that many who entered those cells, convicted or suspected felons, touched by the proofs of sympathy and the words of kindness and the prayer of faith, have been melted and won. Countenances brutalized by indulgence have been awed into reverence, and lips familiar with oaths have learned to breathe the language of devotion; and men who have come outcasts from social sympathies have gone forth redeemed and regenerated. I can testify to the large, liberal, and untiring interest which the late Sheriff manifested on this subject; how he obtained the necessary acts of legislation; how he procured the appointment of a chaplain, selected from his own library moral and religious books, and afforded his hearty co-operation to a band of devoted teachers, who voluntarily gave their sabbath morning's hour to the services of the prisoners. How noble, whole-hearted, and disinterested was his whole bearing there, remote alike from all chilling reserve and all vexatious interference! He might have gone there at stated seasons simply as the minister of the law, and, by means of bar and bolt, have accomplished all that the law required; but he went rather as the minister of mercy. He never relaxed a single rule of the prison; he was stern in the execution of every duty; yet so gentle was he, and considerate towards all, that he never lost the respect and affection of any. He would dash into the midst of an excited mob, where blood was flowing, seize the offender in the midst of his reckless companions, and quell the tumult by a single word; and yet, when compelled to execute the sad sentence of the law, he would weep over the awful necessity, and employ another hand to do what he had not the heart to do by his own. In the way of duty, I have no doubt he would march to the cannon's mouth; yet he would walk the wards, and perform the ungrateful task of the jailor, with a woman's tenderness. He would awe the most hardened by a look, and still the most abandoned by a wave of his hand; yet, when the clergyman chanced to be absent, he would read the sermon with the meekness and solemnity of one born at the altar and for the pulpit. He won the regards of his associates, and reciprocated most sincerely the feelings which he awakened. He was often heard to express the deep satisfaction which the gift of a Bible, a token of personal regard, from the teachers of the Sunday-school in the prison, afforded him. Coming from members of a communion differing from his own, it was peculiarly grateful to him. He won the affections also of the prisoners. Through him they became prisoners of hope. Among those who mourn because this staff of strength is broken, and this rod of beauty, none will mourn more sincerely than they.

Let me offer one more illustration, perhaps it is the most striking of all, of the peculiarities of Col. Lincoln. I refer to the noble act, for which he will be remembered longest, and for which, when his other good deeds are forgotten, he will receive the tribute of the widow's gratitude and the orphan's tears. Bear in mind who and what he was, and then behold the strength of his purpose and the goodness of his heart. He had never experienced the bitterness of orphanage; he had been nursed in plenty. He had never had a wife, — had never looked upon the face, or wept over the loss, of a child. Stern duties called him away into scenes where childhood never enters; yet who among us was touched with so warm a sympathy for the houseless and homeless of our city? Who gave so largely, and furnished with such hearty good-will the "Home" which opens wide its doors, and affords the shelter of its roof to the neglected and forsaken? When our benevolent ladies, successors of those who adorned the early annals of our faith, true Sisters of Charity, had gone out into the streets and gathered together the orphaned, had fed the hungry, clothed the naked, and nursed the sick; and now, exhausted of their resources, appealed to our compassion, — when the poor children

> "Looked up with their pale and sunken faces,
> And their looks were sad to see;
> Your old earth, they say, is very dreary;
> Our young feet, they say, are very weak!" —

who heard this cry, and responded most nobly to this appeal? It was our kind-hearted friend, whose heart has now ceased to beat, and whose hand has done its last work of kindness. He heard the cry, and responded most nobly to the appeal, — not by words of pity, — not by expressions of sympathy, — not by communicating his thought or his feeling to any one on earth. That was not his way. He never told you how much he loved you, nor how much he was interested in any given object; but he dropped the token of his affection in your path, left the gift before the altar, and went his way. So, when he looked upon the pale and sunken faces of these children; when he learned how much had been done for them, and what were now their great needs, — he did not express aloud his pity, and proclaim his purpose, but went to work to provide a spacious home, personally directed all the arrangements, personally procured what in his judgment was most suitable and needful, and then as quietly and unostentatiously recorded his deed of gift, and placed it in the hands of the guardians of the institution; thus, in the surest and most substantial way, laying the foundations of an asylum which will be a glory in our city, and providing a home for the homeless in all time.

From these incidents in the life of our deceased fellow-worshipper, I think it will be easy to obtain some conception of what he was. He was a strong man, — one of the strongest, if not the strongest, we have had among us. Not perhaps in eloquent speech or power of expression, for he was not gifted in that way; though when he spoke he was listened to with attention, for he had something to say. Not perhaps in pre-eminent sagacity, though he was clear-headed and far-sighted: he could look quite through a subject, and knew how to adapt means to ends. The mental quality which distinguished him above all others was an amazing executive talent, an unsurpassed ability to accomplish what he undertook. Nothing seemed too arduous for him to attempt, or too difficult for him to achieve: if it were practicable for any one, he would accomplish it. But with his energy there was no restlessness, no nervous excitability. His step was measured, and his language deliberate. His was a calmness, a tranquillity, but withal a decisiveness, as if the time for argument were over, and the time for action had come. Some who knew him little, called this obstinacy, self-will; and perhaps at times it was, for the oak is gnarled, not the poplar. But others, who knew him better, said it was only a firm reliance on his own clear judgment, and an invincible purpose, which no threats nor entreaties could divert, to follow his convictions of duty. There was within him a deep internal principle of right, and he could no more disregard this than he could deny his own being. During his last sickness, in a half-conscious state, — one of those moods of the spirit induced by his great bodily weakness, — he expressed what I would now indicate as most significant of himself: "Be sure," he said, "you are right, and then go ahead."

This principle of right was also the groundwork of his moral character. He could not do a mean or dishonest act. I never heard his integrity doubted, or the purity of his motives called in question. He was tried by the reverses of fortune. He met with losses; his prospects were overcast, and his affairs involved by the failure of others. He was tried by the harder trial of prosperity. He enjoyed the confidence of friends and the public, and obtained the gratification of his most ambitious desires. But, alike in storm and sunshine, in prosperity and adversity, he was the same man. No extravagance was remembered against him in the days of his success; no mean evasions were charged against him in the season of his reverses. Simple and inexpensive in his habits, trusted and honored alike under each changing circumstance, he himself remained unchanged, — never unduly elated, never unduly depressed. He sought to be faithful where the Providence of God placed him. With each day came the duty and the trial; and in no condition of trial did he find an apology for a neglect of the duty. When he was very sick, the relative who constantly attended him proposed to remain with him, instead of going abroad, on the usual day devoted to some work of charity. But no! feeble as he was, scarcely able to lift his hand, he reminded her of the day and of the work, earnestly adding, "Never neglect a duty." He never neglected his.

But this principle of right, which formed the groundwork of his character, was not an abstraction. It had a foundation in something deeper than itself, — in a profound sentiment of reverence, which seemed to give a coloring to his whole nature, and to pervade his whole being. He revered this, the city of his birth. Every object in the landscape, every relic of its former days, every token of its prosperity, its good name and good estate, were dear to him. These hills were dear because he had looked on them so long; these woods and fields and streams, because they were associated with the aspirations of his youth; and these noble structures for the public use, because they were a part of the labors of his life. He revered the large company of his kindred and friends, the friends of his childhood, and his father's friends; and, once loving, he was unyielding in his attachments, faithful in his friendships, even unto death. Obstinate in his prejudices, never strong in the profession, he was never stinted in the tokens of his attachment. He did not proclaim how dear the city was to him; but everywhere, in the field and in the market, in the grateful shade of the trees by day, and in the brilliancy of the lamps by night, he gave proofs of his regard. He never told his friends how much he loved them; but they were left to infer, by little acts of kindness constantly repeated, by a compliance with their wishes promptly afforded, how much they were on his heart. He had a deep reverence for things sacred, — for the sabbath, for the sanctuary, for the Scriptures, for Christ, and for God. The sentiment was unaffected and profound. Perhaps its very depth prevented an expression through the ordinances, which he might well have given. This I am sure of, — he would not be suspected of professing what he did not feel: he did feel more than he professed. When he was in health, he was always here on the sabbath, forenoon and afternoon. His bearing was always reverential. What was said of Priestley might be said of him, that, when he took the name of God upon his lips, whose presence he recognized by day, and whose guardianship by night, it was with an emotion of awe. He paused ere he uttered the word. It was not in his nature to talk of himself, of his hopes or his fears. During his long sickness, he made no confessions, but evinced his filial trust by the unequalled patience with which he bore his excruciating and protracted pains. Dying, he proclaimed his fitness for the world to which he has gone, by the scrupulous fidelity with which, to the very last, he discharged the duties of the world in which he lived.

And so he is gone. The strong staff is broken, and the beautiful rod. He who has been so long associated with the affairs of this city, county, and commonwealth, — he whose fertile mind projected, and whose prompt energy carried to their completion, so many measures of public utility, — he whose good name was a public property, and whose presence in the midst of us gave a sense of protection, — the good citizen, the faithful friend, the devout fellow-worshipper, — is gone. Gone the man of enterprise, of a strong will and a large heart! He has disappeared from our public assemblies, the places of business, and the retirements of his home. He has been borne from these portals to our garden of sepulchres; and there was mourning, and a great multitude attended his burial. His body now lies in the bosom of the earth which he loved to till, while the awed and trusting spirit has gone up with its account to the God that gave it.

Softly, then, may the turf lie upon that heart; for it had wide and generous sympathies. Gently now fall the leaves of autumn upon that new-made grave; for he who sleeps there dealt not harshly, but kindly with all. Hallowed the dust which reposes there; for he who tenanted it was reverential and devout. To-day our thoughts and affections cluster around it, sad and sorrowing. To-morrow, ay, when seasons have come and gone, silent forms will gather there, and breasts will heave and eyes be suffused with tears, as that manly frame and honest countenance revive in their recollection. The friend will linger there to dwell upon him whose friendship never failed, and the stranger to bless him who did so much to relieve the hard labors of the field, to reclaim the waywardness of his youth, and to provide a home for his orphanage in childhood. Ever fragrant the memory which is embalmed in good deeds, — ever fresh the savor of his name, which is inscribed by a loving service on living hearts.

Meanwhile, let us thank God that he has been among us, and was enabled to accomplish so much in his day and generation. His errors, whatever they were, let them be buried. But let his virtues and his good services be recorded here for the comfort and solace of his surviving kindred; for the grateful contemplation of the old, who were his cotemporaries; and for the encouragement and incitement of the young, who hasten to occupy the places and receive the trusts which he has left. The mention of the righteous shall not fail; they shall be in everlasting remembrance.

APPENDIX.

PROCEEDINGS OF THE WORCESTER LIGHT INFANTRY COMPANY IN RELATION TO THE DEATH OF COL. LINCOLN.

At the monthly meeting of the Worcester Light Infantry, held on the 6th instant, the following resolutions were adopted: —

"*Resolved*, That the Worcester Light Infantry receive the melancholy announcement of the decease of Col. John W. Lincoln, a past commander, with feelings of the deepest regret.

"*Resolved*, That in him were combined all the qualities of gentleman, citizen, and soldier. Always affable and courteous as a gentleman, honest, kind, and public-spirited as a citizen, and firm and patriotic as a soldier, his acquaintances deplore the loss of a most agreeable companion, the community an efficient and devoted member, and we a firm friend, benevolent patron, and most respected past commander.

"*Resolved*, That, under all circumstances, he has been the firm and consistent friend of the military system, laboring for its advancement and perfection with a characteristic devotion. That in him a bright star has fallen from the military constellation, and a firm pillar been taken from the militia edifice; but the consolation remains, that his 'good deeds live after him,' which neither time nor circumstances can sully, but shall shine with increasing lustre as time advances.

"*Resolved*, That we sympathize deeply with the many friends of the deceased, and will wear the customary military badges of mourning.

"Per Order of W. L. I."

RESOLUTIONS OF THE STOCKHOLDERS OF THE WORCESTER BANK.

At the annual meeting of Stockholders of the Worcester Bank on Friday last, the decease of Hon. John W. Lincoln, a member of the Board of Directors, to which he was first elected on the 5th of October, 1829, having been announced, —

"*Voted*, That the Stockholders of the Worcester Bank hold in grateful remembrance the long and faithful services of the late Hon. John W. Lincoln, as one of the Directors of said Bank, and would record their high sense of his character as a man, justly honored by his fellow-citizens for his distinguished ability and moral worth; and would hereby tender their sympathies to the family of the deceased.

"*Voted*, That a copy of the foregoing, duly authenticated, be communicated to the family of the deceased, and be offered for publication to the several newspapers printed in this city.

" From the Records of the Stockholders,

" William Cross, Clerk.

"Worcester, Oct. 11, 1852."

AGRICULTURAL NOTICES.

The following resolutions were adopted at the annual festival of the Worcester West Agricultural Society, a few days before his death: —

" *Resolved*, That the members of this Society have received, with the most unfeigned sorrow, intelligence that the protracted illness from which the Hon. John W. Lincoln has been suffering, is hourly expected to terminate in the death of that eminent citizen and distinguished friend of agriculture.

" *Resolved*, That to him, as much or more than any other man, have the great interests of agriculture in our county and commonwealth been indebted; and that we, the members of the Worcester County West Agricultural Society, extend to him, while yet he lingers with us, our warmest thanks for his valuable contributions to and devoted labors in this most important branch of human industry."

At a meeting of the Trustees of the Worcester Agricultural Society, held in Worcester, on Thursday, the 7th day of October, A. D. 1852, it was —

" *Resolved,* That the Trustees of the Worcester County Agricultural Society lament with unfeigned sorrow the death of Hon. John Waldo Lincoln, their honored and beloved President.

" *Resolved,* That to his efforts and industry much is due for the success with which the affairs of the Society have been heretofore conducted.

" *Voted,* That said Resolutions be recorded by the Secretary on the books of this Board.

A copy, " WM. S. LINCOLN, Rec. Sec."

From a thorough article on the life and services of Col. Lincoln, in the " New England Farmer," the following are extracted: —

" In no department of labor had Col. Lincoln been more useful than in his devotion to the interests of agriculture; and, in later life, his desire for the promotion of agricultural improvement amounted to no less than a ruling passion. . . . He distinguished himself by the science and practical skill with which he employed irrigation. . . . In improvements in breeds of agricultural animals, he was among the foremost of his cotemporaries. Various experiments were in progress upon his farm at the time of his decease, which, had he lived to carry them out, would have elicited important facts contributing to the settlement of some mooted questions in agriculture. Among the improvements he intended to enter upon this present season was the employment of a competent chemist, to make a full analysis of the different soils composing his farm, so that afterwards modes of culture might be adopted which are fitted to the capabilities and wants of each field. . . . Two years ago, he succeeded his worthy brother, Ex-Gov. Lincoln, in the office of President of the Worcester County Agricultural Society. He immediately showed his talent at originating important measures, by putting on foot some experiments, in the name of the Society, calculated to throw light on undetermined matters in agriculture; and he had mostly matured other plans of operation for the Society, which, in their practical workings and results, would unquestionably have proved useful, and commanded very general attention among agriculturalists throughout the country."

It may be added to this, that an essay of Col. Lincoln on the feeding of cattle had a wide circulation among agriculturalists in this country, and was deemed of such distinguished merit that it was republished in England.

WORCESTER COUNTY PRISON.

"Under the superintendence of the late High Sheriff Lincoln, it is well known that the prison and its management had been placed on a basis approaching as near to perfection as such an institution can well be. Every thing about the establishment is indicative of the excellence of his administration.

"In the prison chapel last sabbath morning, as on every sabbath morning, were assembled the inmates of the institution, — all of them tidily and cleanly dressed, and all intent upon the exercises of the occasion. The school ordinarily numbers about seventy, classed under the instruction of some fifteen teachers." — *Daily Transcript, Aug.* 21, 1851.

The following is the letter accompanying the presentation of the Bible referred to in the text: —

"Worcester, Aug. 11, 1851.

"Hon. John W. Lincoln, late Sheriff of the County of Worcester.

"Dear Sir, — The undersigned, teachers in the Sabbath-school in the county prison, ask the privilege to leave with you, on your retirement from your official connection with the institution, and particularly with the Sabbath-school, over which you have so long and so faithfully exercised a supervision, some slight testimonial of the high consideration in which we hold your well-directed efforts in that department of your public trust, as well as your personal friendship; and we can bring to our minds nothing which we deem more appropriate than the Bible.

"Accept then, dear sir, at our hands, this 'precious treasure.' It is the 'best gift,' in our estimation, which we can offer you; and, with it, permit us to offer you the assurance that our prayers for you will be, that the good which you have done, and may yet be instrumental in accomplishing, may be had in 'everlasting remembrance.'

"Truly and respectfully yours,

"Nathan Muzzy,	William P. Smith,
Henry Griffin,	Enoch Hall,
Levi Clapp,	Edward Bemis,
John P. Baker,	Simeon Clapp,
Ichabod Washburn,	Lee Sprague,
John Cheney,	A. G. Wood,
Moses Brigham,	Jonathan Cary."

ORPHANS' HOME.

By a deed dated Nov. 24, 1851, Col. Lincoln made a gift to the Worcester Children's Friends' Society, for their perpetual use, of his estate on Pine-street, valued at about five thousand dollars.

www.ingramcontent.com/pod-product-compliance
Lightning Source LLC
LaVergne TN
LVHW021201120826
845150LV00011B/2340

* 9 7 8 1 4 1 8 1 9 4 9 1 8 *